CLEVELAND RADIO PLAYERS

Published by Cleveland Radio Players

Copyright © 2015 by Milton Matthew Horowitz

All rights, including the right of reproduction in whole or in part, in any form, including digital reproduction, are reserved. Published in the United States by Cleveland Radio Players.

CAUTION: Professionals and amateurs are hereby warned that *Grief Parade*, being fully protected under the Copyright Laws of the United States is subject to royalty. All rights, including professional, amateur, motion picture, recitation, lecturing, public reading, radio and television broadcasting, and the rights of translation into foreign languages, are strictly reserved. Particular emphasis is laid on the question of readings, permission for which must be secured in writing from the author's representative at Cleveland Radio Players, 2218 Superior Ave, Suite 203, Cleveland, OH 44114. The amateur acting rights of *Grief Parade* are controlled exclusively for the author by the author's representative.

ISBN 978-0692462867 (Cleveland Radio Players, The)

Original Adaption and Performances

Originally adapted for the radio and performed by The Cleveland Radio Players. Directed by Milton Matthew Horowitz. Recorded at Bad Racket Studios.

Starring:
(in order of appearance)

Logan Smith	Death
Robert Branch	Everett
Rachel Drake	Jessica

The Grief Parade

By

Cutler Smith

© The Cleveland Radio Players theradioplayers@gmail.com

For rights and royalties please visit:
clevelandradioplayers.com

2218 Superior Ave suite #203
Cleveland Ohio 44114

216 269 4171

ACT 1

> **THE VOICE OF THE CLEVELAND RADIO PLAYERS**
> Hello ... this is the voice of the Cleveland Radio Players... My name is Denny Castiglione Ladies and Gentlemen...

> **OPENING FAN FAIR**
> and you're listening to the Cleveland Radio Players performance of The Grief Parade... Written By Cutler Smith... Directed By Milton Matthew Horowitz... Narrated by Cutler Smith...

SCENE 1

> **FADE IN SUSPENSE MUSIC**

> **DEATH**
> So here's how it happened: On the shoulder of a lonely road, on a gray day, clouds everywhere. And there's a mouse-colored man. He stands alone. He's stopped still at the base of a tall tree, and it's alone also. And our man, he's clutching a black bouquet in his hairy hands. His head is hung, so his chin's in his chest, and he's talking straight down. And this is what he says, he says:

> **FADE OUT SUSPENSE MUSIC**
> **FADE IN CURB SIDE ROAD ENVIRONMENT**

> **EVERETT**
> I'm not sure what I'm supposed to say. I'm not sure if I should... You know I miss you. Or, maybe you don't know it. But I do, babe, everyday. And I love you. I wish... I guess I wish I'd told you more. When I could've told you... when it would've mattered. Seems now you didn't know it enough. (pause) What are you supposed to say?

> **CAR PASSING**
> **FADE OUT ENVIRONMENT**
> **FADE IN SUSPENSE MUSIC**

                    DEATH
               (v.o.)
     And I come upon this scene as I'm
     walking the road. I see this floral
     fella discoursing with a tree
     trunk. I think I see a tear roll
     down his cheek. And I want to say
     something to him, something
     like: 'Don't cry, fella.' But
     because I see no reason why this
     man shouldn't be crying, I don't
     say that, instead. Instead, I say,
     'Hi there.' To which he replies:

               FADE OUT SUSPENSE MUSIC
                              FADE IN ENVIRONMENT

                    EVERETT
     Fine, thanks.

                    DEATH
     (pause) What?

                    EVERETT
     What?

                    DEATH
     You just said, fine thanks. I
     didn't ask you how you were.

                    EVERETT
     Sorry, I misheard you. What was it
     you asked me?

                    DEATH
     I didn't ask you anything. I just
     said 'Hi', didn't I?

                                                   CAR PASSES

                    EVERETT
     Sorry, I thought you might've asked
     me how I was.

                    DEATH
     I didn't.

                    EVERETT
     Well-

                    DEATH
     I didn't ask you how you are. I
     can see how you
     are. (pause) Well?

EVERETT
Well, what?

DEATH
Now that you know what I said, now that you know I said hello to you, aren't you going to say hello to me?

EVERETT
Yeah, sure. Hello.

DEATH
Well, it's a little late for that, isn't it? We've just been talking for the last little while. It's a little late for hello. (pause) So, how are you?

EVERETT
I'm fine-

DEATH
You're fine.

EVERETT
Yes.

DEATH
Right, you said so. (pause) Me too. Yeah, I'm fine. 'Case you were wondering.

CAR PASSES

EVERETT
Oh? Wonderful, look-

DEATH
Is this, uh... this your car here?

EVERETT
Yeah, it's mine.

DEATH
Right! And what's the matter with her?

EVERETT
There's nothing-

DEATH
Is it engine trouble? Gah! That's some of the worst kinda trouble.

EVERETT
No-

DEATH
Then it's gotta be something else. That's a bit of good news. Something else I can fix.

EVERETT
You don't get it-

DEATH
Jesus, what?

EVERETT
There's nothing wrong with the engine, or with anything, it's all alright. The car's fine.

DEATH
You're sure?... It's no trouble. Cars are something I know something about. See, I grew up around cars. Yeah, and all my life it's been cars...

EVERETT
Listen, the car is fine. I'm fine. Everything's fine here, so...

DEATH
It isn't out of gas, is it?

EVERETT
No, it's not out of gas! I just stopped it.

DEATH
Oh, you just... 'Cause I was gonna say, the next gas station is... But you just stopped it. Alright, well... I'd better be, uh... (pause) You're sure you're alright?

EVERETT
Perfectly.

DEATH
Right, well. Goodbye then-

FOOTSTEPS AWAY

EVERETT
Good-bye.

CAR PASSES
WIND IN THE TREES
FOOTSTEPS COMMING CLOSER

DEATH
It's just, I wonder what you're doing all stopped up if you're alright. Most people, they're alright, they'll just keep on moving... on down the road. So, what are you doing? Are you taking a leak?

EVERETT
No, I'm not taking a leak... Not that it's any of your business.

DEATH
I'm just thinking, why's a fella go and stop up on the side of the road? First thing I think is, maybe he's having car trouble. Which, you already said, you haven't got. Next thing I think is, probably he's just stopped to have a little leak. (pause) Uh, but...

EVERETT
But, I wasn't. So...

DEATH
That's right. As you said already. (pause) So... what are you doing? All stopped up?

EVERETT
Look, there's loads and loads of reasons why a person pulls their car over on the side of road! Aren't there? Should we enumerate them? Could be that they're feeling a bit pinched, and they just want to stretch out a bit. Could be that they don't like to eat and drive... cause it always

                    EVERETT
makes a mess... and so they're
stopping to have a picnic for
themselves. It could be that
someone's giving them a
ring-a-ding-ding, and they pull
over to take the call... fearing
that, otherwise, they'd crash
head-on into a van full of golden
orphans! Okay? They could be
particularly sensitive to the
beauty of the place. I mean-

                    DEATH
Only, things are looking
mostly... Yeah, dreary and gray.
Looks like it might rain soon,
even. (shivers) Not really the time
to stop and take it all in, is it?
I mean... yeah, no, not even if
you'd never seen the thing before.
Have you been here before?

                    EVERETT
I've passed by.

                    DEATH
Can't really see much of anything
now, anyhow... what with all the
gray. Still, you're not missing
much. It's a shitty view of nothing
good. Would you like a cigarette?

                    EVERETT
Oh, uh, no. Thanks. I've given up.

                    DEATH
Oh, good for you. I'm not kidding,
good for you. You know, I tried to
quit once.

                    EVERETT
That right?

                    DEATH
Yeah, chewed the gum.

                    EVERETT
Oh yeah? And, what, you didn't like
it?

                    DEATH
No, I liked it fine... yeah, loved
it, actually. No, it worked a
wonder there. When I quit it was on
the spot, on the spot. If I wanted
a cigarette, I'd chew on my gum for
a bit. Always did the trick.

                    EVERETT
Oh. But...

                    DEATH
What?

                    EVERETT
Well, I mean... you did start back
up again.

                    DEATH
Well, what happened was, I got into
such a good thing with the
quitter's gum, I near raped myself
poor financing my chewing habit. Do
you know what it costs you, the
gum?..goddamn fortune. In the end,
it was a financial
decision. (pause) And thinking of
it now... I mean, because it was a
financial thing and not an
addiction thing... Technically. I
still quit.

                    EVERETT
What?

                    DEATH
Don't you think? Technically? I
mean, because it wasn't that I
needed the cigarettes back in my
life. Wasn't that I couldn't get
along without them. I did. I
could've said goodbye to cigarettes
forever. The gum and I, we were
very happy together. It's just that
the gum was costing me a goddamn
fortune. See, my will was very
strong. I've a very strong will.
Fucking granitic will. A will like
you wouldn't believe. Alright,
let's have it, what's with the
flowers?

                    EVERETT
Oh. These? They're just-

                    DEATH
Wait, don't tell me! You picked
them! And you stopped here to pick
flowers, am I right?

                    EVERETT
No.

                    DEATH
Oh.

                    EVERETT
No. Do you see any flowers around?

                    DEATH
You could've picked them.

                    EVERETT
All of them? And, what, there just
happened to be about a bouquet?

                    DEATH
So, who are they for? Wait, don't
tell me! You've pissed off your
lady, am I right? She's screaming
pissed, so you're bringing her
flowers. What'd you do? Or... wait,
but then you wouldn't have to stop.

                    EVERETT
Do you know how sometimes, as
you're traveling, you'll sometimes
see a spot on the side of the road
where people have brought a lot of
candles, and pictures, and flowers
and things?

                    DEATH
Oh, like for when someone's died
there?

                    EVERETT
Yeah, like for when someone's died
there.

                    DEATH
Well, sure, you see 'em all the
time.

                              FADE ROAD SIDE SOUNDS

                    DEATH
                (v.o.)
          with that the man takes up his
          flowers, regards em, and, without
          looking, tosses them at the
          tree. He missed. Whiffed. But I
          took his meaning.

                              FADE IN ROAD SIDE SOUNDS

                    DEATH
          Oh... Is this spot one of those
          spots?

                    EVERETT
          Yeah.

                    DEATH
          Huh. (pause) I never understood
          that kind of thing, myself.

                    EVERETT
          What do you mean? What don't you
          understand? It's what you do. When
          someone you love dies on the side
          of the road, it's what you do.

                    DEATH
          I don't know, just seems so... no,
          never mind.

                    EVERETT
          No, just seems so, what? What were
          you going to say?

                    DEATH
          Well, it just seems like... like a
          bit of a waste, really. Yeah, all
          those flowers and pictures and
          things.

                    EVERETT
          It's not a waste! It's a symbol.

                    DEATH
          I just don't see the point, is all-

                    EVERETT
          It's a symbolic-fucking-gesture...
          you don't see the... ? The point is
          that someone's dead. Someone, some
          loved-one, has ceased to exist on
          the side of the road. And so the

                    EVERETT
          point is to make it look a little
          less like an ordinary
          fucking-stretch of fucking-road!

                    DEATH
          (pause) Only... it is an ordinary
          stretch of road.

                                                  CAR PASSES

                    EVERETT
          It isn't an ordinary stretch of
          road! It's part of an ordinary
          stretch of road where something
          really important happened.
          (pause) Might even be that the
          most important thing that can
          happen to a person, happened to a
          person right here. And, sure,
          shouldn't the place be made to look
          a little more important?

                    DEATH
          I don't know...

                    EVERETT
          What'd'you mean, you don't know?

                    DEATH
          Well, just cause someone's died,
          that's no reason to go building a
          shrine about it. Don't people die
          all over the place? Now, if
          everyone decided that decorating
          was the only appropriate response,
          why, the world'd be overrun with
          decorations. Besides, isn't it
          littering?

                    EVERETT
          No, it's isn't... Littering?

                    DEATH
          You're sure?

                    EVERETT
          What? They're flowers.

                    DEATH
          Well, sure, the flowers don't
          count. But the rest of it. The
          candles, and the pictures, and all
          that. The detritus.

EVERETT
They're so that, then, at least there's a trace. They're mementos.

DEATH
I'm just saying, they don't break down as fast.

EVERETT
They're not supposed to! That's the whole thing!

DEATH
I mean, why not just bring all that paraphernalia round to the grave, anyway? You'd think most people'd want to dump it there, and be keeping up with the Jones's.

EVERETT
It's a monument. It's for everyone. To let everyone know, someone's-

DEATH
Oh, fuck off is it for everyone! I could've gone by just now thinking, my, what a nice tree. Shady. And instead you've got me thinking, this tree, that I thought was nice, is actually an instrument of DEATH. Your flowers. But, hang on... where is everything else?

EVERETT
What do you mean?

DEATH
Where's all the other tacky crap? It's just your flowers here.

EVERETT
So?

DEATH
So, either you're the first of your grieving-kind, or, your dead friend was a bit of a bastard.

EVERETT
How about, you just shut up about it. Alright?

DEATH
Alright, hey, easy-

EVERETT
You didn't know her.

DEATH
Okay, you're right, I didn't know her-

EVERETT
She was... well, she...

DEATH
I'm sure. I'm sure she was... quite a lady!

EVERETT
Hey! She was quite a lady.

DEATH
And I'm sure she was. It's why I'm wondering, how come it's just your flowers sitting up for her?

EVERETT
Well, it just happened.

DEATH
Oh, really? Hm. You know, you wouldn't be able to tell, this tree hasn't got a mark on it... it's really unbelievable. When did you say it happened?... oh, my god!

EVERETT
Five days ago... what is it?

DEATH
There's a spot.

EVERETT
There's a spot?

DEATH
Right there. Is that mud, or is it blood?

EVERETT
Oh, my god... oh, my god, it's probably blood-

DEATH
Hm. Just mud, I guess... five days? You sure did take your time getting up here.

EVERETT
What'd'you expect-

DEATH
Five days!

EVERETT
I was grieving, wasn't I? They didn't even have the funeral until today. Probably going on right now.

DEATH
Well, why aren't you there? That's where the action is. Sometimes, there's a point in the service... you know, and they're being lowered into the ground... and everyone stands round the hole chucking dirt clods at the casket.

EVERETT
Alright, fucker, I'm warning you. Watch it. You're talking about my wife.

DEATH
Oh, so, it's your wife that died knocked into this tree?

EVERETT
Yes.

DEATH
Oh...

EVERETT
And anyway... I couldn't bring myself to do it, the service. I couldn't face them.

DEATH
Who couldn't you face?

EVERETT
Forget it. (pause) Let's just say, not everyone in her family was... some of them weren't that fond of me, is all.

DEATH
Your mother-in-law, then?

EVERETT
... The bitch.

DEATH
It's always the mother-in-law. I wonder why that is. What's it with your mother-in-law? What'd you do?

EVERETT
Nothing. I was a very good son-in-law. I was a good husband.

DEATH
Well, of course you were. Yeah, and I'll bet it's the last thing that went through her head, too... before she died... how good you always were to her. Probably she was comforted by that. (pause) You know, apart from that one thing, funerals don't have much going for them. I doubt you're missing much. Oh! hey, have you heard of these Life-Gems? They've thought up a way to turn a person's ashes into a wee little jewel... a precious little people-jewel. And you can set them in a ring, or a locket, or on the mantle under glass. There's also a way to have the ashes loaded into a round of ammunition. (pause) Shit, can't remember what that's called. Burial's probably the least interesting way to go. I mean, when you think about all the other options available... in this age of godless confusion, and technological innovation-

EVERETT
What's going on here?

DEATH
What'd'you mean?

EVERETT
Why am I still talking to you? You probably have something to do today, right? How about, you go do that? I'd like to be alone here for a while. With the tree.

                    DEATH
Fine... Fine, yeah, I suppose I'll
leave you to it. This conversation
was lacking, anyway. And, you're
right I've got loads to do. So...
Goodbye.

                                FADE OUT ENVIRONMENT

                    DEATH
                      (v.o.)
And I was going to walk away. I
was just going to turn, audience
and go. But something stops
me. Something like...

                                FADE IN ENVIRONMENT

                    DEATH
Actually, untrue. I've got nothing
else to do. So, your wife, huh?
That must be terrible. Is it
terrible?

                    EVERETT
Would you please just get the fuck
out of here?

                    DEATH
Wouldn't it be weird if I knew her?
Was your wife Brandi?

                    EVERETT
No-

                    DEATH
Or, Janine?

                    EVERETT
No-

                    DEATH
I'm just guessing people I know.
Was her name Angelica?... Angie?

                    EVERETT
No! look, would you-

                    DEATH
Just, give me one more guess. Was
her name... Jessica?

                    EVERETT
          (pause)
A lot of people are named Jessica.

                    DEATH
But she is one of them? Aha! look
at me go. Do you see what a good
guesser I am?

                    EVERETT
Yes, you're very good-

                    DEATH
Alright, now, let's see if I can't
guess her last name...

                    EVERETT
          (quietly)
I hate you so much-

                    DEATH
Was it... Postman? (pause) No need
to say anything, I take it from
your lack of response that I've hit
the proverbial nail on the fucking
head. Jessica Postman.

                    EVERETT
How could you know that?

                    DEATH
I didn't, it was just a good
guess. Just a wild guess.

                    EVERETT
Oh yeah? Or are you fucking with
me?

                    DEATH
No, hey-

                    EVERETT
Did you know my wife?

                    DEATH
No, honest, I don't even know a
Jessica Postman. I know a Jessica,
I don't know a Jessica Postman.
That Postman-thing really was a
shot in the dark... was one in a
million, really. (pause) I'm not
fucking with you! Truly. If I was
fucking with you, wouldn't I have

DEATH
rather let slip some more intimate detail? Which, of course, I couldn't actually do... since I didn't actually know your wife. (pause) Jessica Postman.

EVERETT
Okay.

DEATH
Yeah, no. If I'd said something like, the last time you and Jessica slept in the same bed was one month and five days ago... I'd just be hazarding a guess... I wouldn't be fucking with you.

EVERETT
(pause)
How did you know that?

DEATH
Well, it's obvious, isn't it? Either, I'm omniscient, or, your wife had a close male friend and confidant of whom you knew absolutely nothing.

EVERETT
YOU SON OF A--

DEATH
Wait! Wait! (pause) I am omniscient.

EVERETT
What?

DEATH
I swear, I'm not screwing your wife. Please don't hit me. I know all that stuff because I know everything.

EVERETT
(pause)
You're not omniscient!

DEATH
Yes I am, I'm DEATH.

EVERETT
What? You're not DEATH, you couldn't be.

DEATH
Why couldn't I be?

EVERETT
What, you? It's ridiculous.

DEATH
How do you know I'm not DEATH?

EVERETT
Oh, come on, DEATH-personified?

DEATH
Yeah, all right, probably not. But... how can you be sure?

EVERETT
(pause) You're not DEATH. No one would believe it. Have you seen yourself?

DEATH
What do you mean?

EVERETT
What do I mean? Look at the way you're dressed.

DEATH
What's wrong with it?

EVERETT
A little unofficial, aren't we, Mr. DEATH? Come on, you didn't even conjure yourself comfortable shoes. What, did you know my wife from the soup kitchen?

DEATH
Well, if I had come to you... in the fullness and splendor of my theophany... you would have just laughed at me. (pause) I'm fucking with you!

EVERETT
I knew it-

DEATH
No, yeah-

EVERETT
I knew you couldn't be DEATH-

DEATH
Oh. (pause) No, see, I meant about the... my theophany. No, I really am DEATH.

EVERETT
Right, okay. And, what, you're here to end my life, is that it? The end's nigh, right, that's what this means?

DEATH
Maybe.

EVERETT
Maybe?

DEATH
Maybe I'm here to end your life. Maybe it's already over.

EVERETT
Oh, I see. And, I'm dead, then?... just like that? Spooky.

DEATH
I'm just saying, maybe you're dead.

EVERETT
You didn't even do anything!

DEATH
Well, but, who's to say? You and me are the only ones around. (eerily) Do you think you'd know? If you're dead, do you think you know it?

EVERETT
Fuck. You.

DEATH
Come on, we're just chatting. Hypothetically, I'm saying-

EVERETT
We're done chatting. Now, it's time for you to go.

                    DEATH
I'm not going anywhere.

                    EVERETT
You will, or I'll make you. Now, which is it going to be?

                    DEATH
You'll have to make me, then. I have just as much a right to be here as you have... loitering at the base of this tree. Just cause your wife drew her last, when she was slumped up against it... this is still public property. Where are you going?

                    EVERETT
I'm leaving... don't know why I stayed this long.

                    DEATH
Wait! Could you just wait a second! Can I have a ride please?

                    EVERETT
You've got to be kidding-

                    DEATH
I'm not headed far-

                    EVERETT
After all that DEATH bullshit?... so, why don't you walk if you're not headed far?

                    DEATH
Come on, don't be such an asshole.

                    EVERETT
I'm allowed to be an asshole. It's my right to be an asshole, cause you've been such a sonofabitch! I just wanted to be left alone here for a while, to reckon with the gaping hole in my life. You couldn't just leave me to it? Couldn't just pass me by? When you realized... that I didn't stop here... to take a fucking leak!

DEATH
Well, but, if I'd left earlier, I wouldn't be able to catch a ride with you now. So...

EVERETT
Well, you're still not going to catch a ride with me now, you tactless-fucking-psychopath.

FADE OUT ENVIRONMENT

DEATH
(v.o.)
And he made to go. Started stalking away. He was in this great damn huff. I sat down, kicked my heels up and rested my head, I wasn't going anywhere... If this Samaritan was determined to leave me lying on the roadside, it's there that I resolved to stay. So I called out after him.

FADE IN ENVIRONMENT

DEATH
I see. Well, if that's how you feel, yeah, I guess I'll just be sticking around here, then. Probably try and find somewhere to set up camp.

FADE OUT ENVIRONMENT

DEATH
(v.o.)
That brought about some change in him, seemed to change his mind. Because he didn't drive away.

FADE IN ENVIRONMENT

EVERETT
What was that?

DEATH
Oh, here looks good. Yes, I might try camping right here.

                    EVERETT
Why would you want to sleep here,
you just said you weren't headed
far?

                    DEATH
Well, not everyone's been scooting
around all morning in fancy cars.
My feet hurt. (pause) What's the
matter? You look so pensive. You
don't mind me passing the night
here, do you?

                    EVERETT
Yes, I mind! You can't stay here.

                    DEATH
Jesus, what's all the fuss about?
Oh, I know, cause it's a little
like I'm passing the night with the
memory of your missus.

                    EVERETT
You're not staying here!

                              SLEEPING BAG RUSTLING

                    DEATH
Oh, come on, you're taking my
sleeping bag away from me?... (long
pause) ... Who does that?

                    EVERETT
Well, who does this... ?

                    DEATH
I'm DEATH.

                    EVERETT
You're not fucking DEATH!

                    DEATH
Yes... I... am. (beat)

                              FADE OUT ENVIRONMENT

                    DEATH
              (v.o.)
It's worth mentioning, I was
armed. I had a gun. And I only
mention this because it's then that
I took it from out of my
pants. And leveled it at him.

FADE IN ENVIRONMENT

EVERETT
Bullshit. That thing isn't loaded.

GUN SHOT

SUSPENSE MUSIC

Why would DEATH need a gun?

DEATH
Well, DEATH wouldn't. That is, if we're talking about DEATH, the abstract force. But I might have just meant that I was a DEATH ... yours. In which case, I need a gun. Now, get down on your knees, EVERETT.

EVERETT
Oh, my god... oh, my god, please don't shoot me!

DEATH
Right, now, before you die, tell me this... did you love your wife?

EVERETT
My wife?

DEATH
That's right, your wife. Did you love her? Do you have to think about it? I've got a gun to your head, I'm about to scatter your brains on the side of the road, you haven't got time to think. Did you love your wife?

EVERETT
Yes!

DEATH
Yeah? How much would you say?

EVERETT
A lot... I loved her a lot!

DEATH
You loved her a lot. Well, was that enough?... or did your wife deserve more love?

EVERETT
She deserved more.

DEATH
Hey... You're fucking right she did. (pause) Alright, now, compare your love to something.

EVERETT
What?

DEATH
Compare it to something. Like, a flower, say: 'My love is like a flower.'

EVERETT
Okay, okay, uh... Fuck, all I can think about now is flowers.

DEATH
You can't say flowers, I already said flowers. You've got to compare it to something else.

EVERETT
Ask me something else.

DEATH
What?

EVERETT
You have to ask me something else.

DEATH
No! No, I don't have to ask you something else. Cause what you were supposed to have said was, 'My love is incomparable.' 'My love for Jessica is beyond compare', is what you were supposed to say.

EVERETT
Please, please, don't kill me!

DEATH
Why shouldn't I kill you? You're a miserable little shit, Everett. You know it, I know it, and the reason you fear your mother-in-law is, she's known all along. The only one who seemed to be blind to that fact was your late wife. And it wasn't

                    DEATH
          that she was blind to it, she just
          happened to adore you despite your
          being such a scummy little man. And
          you, you fucked it all up. Someone
          like you, you're not capable of
          love... and I should shoot you just
          for lying to me!

                                              GUN COCKS

                    EVERETT
          No, please. Look... I know I
          haven't been the best person...
          but, I'm not such a bad person. I'm
          a doctor! I'm a doctor, I help
          people!

                    DEATH
          Are you really? I thought you were
          a psychologist.

                    EVERETT
          What? Psychologists are still
          doctors.

                    DEATH
          Well, yeah, maybe, but its hardly
          the same thing. Psychology's...
          well, it's just a lot of sex and
          violence, isn't it?

                    EVERETT
          Are you going to kill me or aren't
          you?

                    DEATH
          I'd sure like to kill you. Probably
          loads of reasons why you're shit;
          why you deserve to come to a shitty
          end... with your corpse fallen near
          a bouquet of flowers... that are
          only there because you brought em
          yourself. But, Jessica wouldn't've
          wanted it that way. Still, as I
          can't leave her honor entirely
          unavenged...   Stand up, Doc.
             (pause) Hm...   Take your coat off
          for me.

                    EVERETT
          My coat?

DEATH
Your coat, take it off. It's a
handsome coat, and I want it for my
collection... of handsome coats.

RUSTLING CLOTHES

(pause) Right. Now, kick off your
shoes. Throw em over here.

SHOES FLOP OFF

EVERETT
You're serious? You want my shoes,
now?

DEATH
Yes, I think you were right about
mine, they're rags. I'd be much
more comfortable in something like
what you've got there. Give me your
goddamn shoes, before I shoot you
in the head. (pause) Feels like
we're in a hood movie, doesn't it?
A bit? On account of, I robbed you
of your shoes at gunpoint.
(pause) Okay, these fit well
enough. Good. Yeah, I think we're
about square here.

EVERETT
That's it, then? My coat and my
shoes. Sure you don't want my pants
or the shirt off my back, or
anything?

DEATH
Why, should I want your pants? Have
you got, like, really nice pants?

EVERETT
No, I was just-

DEATH
If you want me to wear the pants,
Everett, I can wear the pants. Is
that what you want? No? So, why are
we talking about pants? Toss me the
keys to your car.

EVERETT
What the hell am I supposed to do?
How am I supposed to get home from
here?

DEATH
Oh, geez, I hadn't thought about that. I suppose you'll have to walk, won't you? But, tell you what, I'll give you something to think about along the way. It'll help pass the time. (pause) You know, when your wife died she was on her way to see you. Did you know that? Now, the only reason she would have gone to see you precisely then, is, she had something to tell to you that couldn't wait until you came home. Something far too important. The thing that's given to you to wonder is... what could that have been? What do you think it was... that she wanted to tell you so badly... she couldn't just wait a few more hours? What was that most important thing... that she never... got... to say? Now, start walking.

DEATH
(v.o.)
And he walked away. Sunken, sullen. And at gun point. I watched him as he went. Watching him go, going. And when he was gone, I moved to the tree. I plucked the flowers from the ground and I smelled them: pretty good. It's then that Jessica Postman appeared to me, the raised spirit of her, coming from out of the trunk of the tree. Like a genie, issuing from out of a wooden lamp: it was wonderful, it was like a Disney movie, glorious. And I says to Jessica, I says:

FADE IN ENVIRONMENT

DEATH
Did you hear him, whining to me about his walk home?

JESSICA
I know, I almost feel sorry for the guy. (pause) I think that bit at the end there might've been a

JESSICA
little much... the urgent message... There was no urgent message, you know.

DEATH
Yeah, I know. But now he'll be tearing his hair out in fistfulls wondering what you might have said to him. It's gonna be hilarious. He probably thinks you were pregnant.

JESSICA
I was just going for Chinese food.

DEATH
Yeah, but it makes for a better story if there's this big important something that you never got to say. It's more tragic this way.

JESSICA
I guess so.

DEATH
Oh, no, it is. Trust me. End notes are something I know something about.

CINEMATIC IMPACT
EERIE MUSIC

FADE OUT ALL

-THE END-

CLOSING CREDITS

FADE IN CLOSING FAN FARE

THE VOICE OF THE CLEVELAND RADIO PLAYERS
you have been listening to The Grief Parade ... Written by Cutler Smith... Directed by Milton Matthew Horowitz... Starring...

ROBERT BRANCH

CUTLER SMITH

and

...my name is Denny Castiglione Ladies and Gentlemen... Just Passing Through was recorded in one live take at Bad Racket Studios... to purchase Just passing through in paperback, MP3, or vinyl record please visit www.clevelandradioplayers.com ... copyright 2015

Rights and Royalties

Originally adapted for the radio and performed by The Cleveland Radio Players

Directed by Milton Matthew Horowitz

Recorded at Bad Racket Studios

For more information on performance rights and royalties, or to listen to Grief Parade as a radio play, please visit www.ClevelandRadioPlayers.com